WORDS *of* HOPE *and* HEALING

Too Much Grief:
COPING
with GRIEF
OVERLOAD

Alan D. Wolfelt, Ph.D.

Companion
P R E S S

An imprint of the Center for Loss and Life Transition | Fort Collins, Colorado

Companion Press is an imprint of the Center for Loss and Life Transition, 3735 Broken Bow Road, Fort Collins, Colorado 80526.

25   24   25   22   21   6   5   4   3   2

ISBN: 978-1-61722-287-0

CONTENTS

Welcome 1

What Is Grief Overload? 3

   Tragic incidents 3

   Traumatic loss and grief overload. 4

   Back-to-back losses 5

   Losses other than death 5

   Secondary losses 6

   Cumulative losses 7

   Grief overload in the elderly .7

   Caregiver grief overload 8

   My grief overload 9

Complicated Grief. 11

What You May Think and Feel .13

   Numbing and disconnection 14

   Denial and avoidance. 15

   Anxiety and fear. 16

   What to do when you're feeling
   very anxious or panicked. 17

   Sadness and depression 19

   Guilt and regret 20

   Anger and other explosive emotions 20

   Relief and release 21

   Physical symptoms. 22

Cognitive symptoms 23

Spiritual symptoms 23

Grief overload and your family 25

Your Six Needs of Mourning. 27

One dose at a time. 28

Grief overload and professional counseling 29

1. Acknowledge the reality of the losses. 29

2. Embrace the pain of the losses. 31

Managing intrusive thoughts and feelings 32

3. Remember the people who died and
   the things you lost 33

4. Develop a new self-identity .34

5. Search for meaning 36

6. Receive ongoing support from others 38

Make a Mourning Plan 41

My mourning plan. 42

Reconciling Your Grief 47

A Final Word 49

Coping with Grief Overload:
The Mourner's Bill of Rights 51

WELCOME

"Grieving is like having broken ribs.
On the outside you look fine, but with every breath, it hurts."
— Author Unknown

If you are feeling overwhelmed by too much loss, this book is for you.

Loss and unwanted change are unavoidable parts of everyone's life, but sometimes we as humans experience a disproportionate number or degree of bad things. Sometimes the losses stack too high, creating a sorrow that seems too great to bear.

In the face of too much loss, it's normal to feel devastated, exhausted, or hopeless. It's normal to feel paralyzed and overburdened. Rest assured that the overwhelming nature of your grief is a normal reaction. What is abnormal is the unusually challenging life situation you are in right now.

Yet there is so much hope. By familiarizing yourself with the basic principles in this compassionate guide, you are already taking a big step toward healing. You see, grief responds to awareness. When you educate yourself about grief and mourning, you are making the experience more understandable and bearable. It becomes something you can work on rather than something that simply happens to you.

I have been a grief counselor and educator for more than forty years now. In my work, and in my own life, I have encountered a great deal of loss. It might help you to know that grief overload is a fairly common, though indeed painful and grueling, circumstance. At one point or another in their lives, many people find themselves dragged under by too much loss.

In fact, I have noticed that more and more of us are becoming grief overloaded because, thanks to medical advances, people are living longer. Where death used to be an everyday occurrence, now it's common for us to live into our 40s or 50s before someone close to us dies—and then, all too often, loved ones start getting sick and dying one after another.

But the overburdened grievers I've learned from have also taught me this: Over time and through active mourning, which we'll discuss in the pages to come, they came through. And so will you.

Thank you for entrusting me to walk beside you on this difficult path.

WHAT IS GRIEF OVERLOAD?

"You give yourself permission to grieve by recognizing the need for grieving."
— Doug Manning

Grief overload is what you feel when you experience too many significant losses all at once or in a relatively short period of time.

The grief of loss overload is different from typical grief because it is emanating from more than one loss and because it is jumbled. Our minds and hearts have enough trouble coping with one loss at a time, but when they have to deal with multiple losses simultaneously, the grief often seems especially chaotic and defeating. Before you can mourn one loss, here comes another loss. Even if you have coped with grief effectively in the past, you may be finding that this time it's different. This time it may feel like you're struggling to survive.

Tragic incidents
Unfortunately, sometimes several people die in a single incident. Natural disasters, car accidents, and acts of violence

can cause the deaths of multiple people you care about all at once. Such traumatic circumstances naturally give rise to grief overload. If you have suffered this type of loss, I urge you to read the section below on traumatic loss. You are in particular need of extra support and care.

TRAUMATIC LOSS AND GRIEF OVERLOAD

All significant losses feel traumatic, but here I want to talk specifically about losses caused by sudden and often violent events. Murder, suicide, and death by a traumatic accident or natural disaster all fall into this category. So do events that cause severe injuries instead of death and/or significant damage to homes and property, such as fires.

Multiple people may die in a traumatic incident, or one person might die and others may be seriously injured. Or no one might die, but several people—including you, perhaps—might be hurt, or maybe your home, belongings, and financial stability might be destroyed.

If you are reading this book because, at least in part, you have suffered a traumatic loss of any kind, you are at risk for your grief overload being influenced by what is called "**traumatic grief**." Traumatic grief is grief that has an added component of intense fear and other challenging symptoms caused by the violent nature of the incident itself.

If flashbacks, memory gaps, persistent negative or intrusive thoughts, low self-esteem, hyper-vigilance or anxiety, personality change, and/or an inability to handle the tasks of daily living are part of your grief overload experience, I urge you to see your primary-care physician and a trauma-trained grief counselor. You will need—and you deserve—extra support and care in addition to the education and self-care guidance offered in this book. You might also find solace and support in my book *The PTSD Solution*, as PTSD and traumatic grief are largely one and the same experience.

Back-to-back losses

Other times, a number of people you love may die of unrelated causes but in quick succession. If a close friend dies of cancer, then a parent dies of natural causes in old age, and then a sibling is killed in an accident, for example, you are certain to feel overwhelmed by too much loss all at once.

These deaths might happen within days or weeks of each other or within months or a few years. But it's also important to note that there are no hard-and-fast deadlines that define grief overload caused by successive loss. If you feel overloaded by grief, no matter how spread out in time the losses have been, you are experiencing grief overload.

Losses other than death

And it's not only death loss that causes grief overload. Other types of significant loss are also common contributors. Whenever you lose something you are or have been attached to, you naturally grieve the change or separation. This means that job loss often causes grief. Divorce causes grief. Health problems cause grief. Estrangement from loved ones causes grief. A move away from a beloved home or location causes grief. When you experience a number of such significant losses in a period of time, in addition to or even in lieu of death losses, you may well find yourself suffering grief overload.

Secondary losses
What's more, secondary losses are also intrinsic components of grief overload. That's because each significant loss in our lives gives rise to a number of related losses, like ripples in a pond after a stone is dropped in.

For example, if a spouse or partner dies, we don't only suffer the loss of that important relationship and unique individual. We also experience related losses, such as the loss of our self-identity as half of a twosome, the loss of our hoped-for future, the potential loss of financial security, and many more. Even everyday life changes resulting from a major loss—such as no longer having a companion to prepare and eat dinner with each night—fall into this category of secondary loss. Secondary losses can make it feel like loss is permeating every aspect of our lives. Everywhere we turn, there's nothing but loss.

Cumulative losses

On a related note, cumulative lifetime losses can also lead to or be a factor in grief overload. Throughout our lives, we all experience loss, of course. From the time we are young, pets die, friendships break, and other hardships present themselves year after year after year. But what you may not realize is that if you don't fully grieve and mourn each loss as it arises, you end up carrying unreconciled grief. Eventually that carried grief can add up and become an unsustainably weighty burden. If you suspect that long-ago losses might be part of your grief overload right now, you're probably right.

Grief overload in the elderly

Finally, older people often find themselves experiencing grief overload for a combination of reasons mentioned above. Increasingly, their friends and peers begin to die in faster succession, their health often deteriorates, and they may have also accumulated a great deal of carried grief over the course of their lives.

If you are an older person affected by grief overload, the principles in this book will help you through this challenging phase of your life and make the most of the precious years you have left. I myself am in my mid-sixties as I write this, and I want you to know that while I understand that loss overload in our final decades is a very real challenge, we can continue to live and love meaningfully as long as we also continue to actively mourn.

CAREGIVER GRIEF OVERLOAD

Professional caregivers of all kinds are at risk for grief overload. If your job, career, or dedicated volunteer role involves helping others who are experiencing trauma or loss of any kind, grief overload is both something to be aware of and something to proactively anticipate and address in your self-care plan.

While professional grief overload and its proper handling is outside the scope of this brief guide, I urge you to read my book *Companioning You: A Soulful Guide to Caring for Yourself While You Care for the Dying and the Bereaved.* Whether you work in a hospice, funeral home, hospital, or school, whether you are a counselor, medical professional, or another type of caregiver altogether, this book will help you identify, prevent, and deal with burnout and grief overload as well as create an action plan for caring for—or companioning—yourself.

MY GRIEF OVERLOAD

I invite you to review pages 3 through 8 then inventory all of the losses—recent, past, and secondary; death-related and non-death-related—that may be contributing to your current experience of grief overload. Please list them here. Identifying the losses you are grieving is the start of creating an action plan to mourn them and heal.

....

....

....

....

....

....

....

....

....

....

....

....

Too Much Loss: Coping with Grief Overload

COMPLICATED GRIEF

*"To embrace one's brokenness, whatever it looks like,
whatever has caused it, carries within it the possibility
that one might come to embrace one's healing."*
— Robert Benson

Grief overload is not a disorder. It's not an illness or abnormality. Instead, it's simply a form of complicated grief.

Of course, all grief is complicated, because it is always complex and multifaceted. It's common for grievers to feel like they're going crazy because their inner experience of loss is so different from their usual, predictable thoughts and feelings.

But grief overload is extra-complicated. It's regular old complicated grief compounded by additional loss and challenging extenuating circumstances. Complicated grief feels more intense. It moves at a slower pace. It requires extra patience, support, and compassion. And it takes longer to heal.

You are experiencing complicated grief. You need and deserve extra patience, support, and compassion. This book will help set you on a healthy path to healing.

WHAT YOU MAY
THINK AND FEEL

"One cannot get through life without pain...What we can do is choose how to use the pain that life presents to us."

— Bernie Siegel

Your grief is the sum total of everything you think and feel as a result of the losses that have contributed to your grief overload.

I'll repeat that grief is always a complex and ever-changing mix of thoughts and feelings, but in cases of grief overload, that mixture gets even more entangled. That's because each loss you've experienced gives rise to its own unique grief response.

The grief you are experiencing about one loss is not precisely the same as the grief you are experiencing about another loss. The two (or more) griefs probably have thoughts and feelings in common, but they also diverge in subtle and pronounced ways. This is normal. Why? Because just as each love and attachment in our lives is unique, each loss and grief is unique as well.

13

The result of this uniqueness is that grief overload tends to cause a kind of snarled, dense, knotted-up grief. It's hard to untangle which thoughts and feelings are associated with which loss. But a key to healing grief overload is to give each unique loss its own time and attention, which we'll be talking about later in this resource.

For now, as you read through the following list of common grief feelings, I want you to think about two things:

1. how you may or may not be experiencing each feeling, and

2. how each feeling may feel subtly or entirely different for each of the unique losses you are grieving.

After we review common feelings, we'll be discussing what to *do* about the feelings.

NUMBING AND DISCONNECTION

In the short-term, nature protects us from the full force of any significant trauma or loss by cocooning us in shock and numbness. Shock and numbness help us survive what would otherwise be unsurvivable. Then, in normal grief, we absorb more and more of the reality of what happened, slowly and over time.

But in cases of grief overload, it's common for grievers to get stuck in numbness and disconnection. A number of grief-overload survivors have described it to me as if they were on the outside of themselves looking in. Is this how you are feeling? If the losses are just too much to absorb, you may perpetually feel numb and unable to get in touch with your truer, deeper feelings. You might feel detached from the world and people around you. You may feel like you're constantly in a daze or a dream-like state.

This response is called "psychic numbing." It protects you from fully feeling your pain, yes, but it also separates you from fully living your life. You may be existing but not really living. As Brené Brown says, "We cannot selectively numb emotions. When we numb the painful emotions, we also numb the positive emotions."

DENIAL AND AVOIDANCE

When something overwhelms us, we tend to avoid it. That's human nature.

In grief overload, it's like you're standing in the surf of a raging ocean, repeatedly getting knocked over and spun around. You're drowning. To save yourself, you might try to crawl out of the waves altogether. This is a normal and life-affirming impulse. You might make your way up the beach and, now that you can breathe again, choose (consciously or unconsciously) not to get back into the water again.

If you're experiencing too much loss, it's understandable to deny or avoid your grief. After all, it's too much to deal with. It's more than any one human can bear. So, to avoid the chaotic pain, you might distract yourself with work, family or household commitments, or mindless activities such as watching TV. Or you might tell yourself that you're doing fine, and whenever any difficult feelings come up, deny them by quickly turning to another task. You also might avoid any places or people who remind you of the losses. Grief overload often gives rise to a "fight, flight, or freeze" response, and avoidance is the "flight" option. You are essentially fleeing the problem because you can't look it in the face.

Like shock and numbness, which are the "freeze" option, denial and avoidance can protect you from drowning in pain…but only for a while. They're healthy responses at first, but eventually they become harmful coping mechanisms that put up a wall between you and anything real and intimate in your life, including relationships with others you care about.

ANXIETY AND FEAR

Loss naturally makes us fearful because it disrupts our feelings of stability. We were enjoying a relative sense of normalcy and calm, and then *wham*—the foundation of our lives cracked. Multiple losses can make it feel as if several devastating, one-on-top-of-the-other earthquakes have shattered our lives, leaving the entire foundation not just shaken but obliterated altogether.

In grief overload, it's normal to fear that something else bad will happen. After all, your life has established a pattern: this happened, then this happened, then this happened…so something else is bound to happen next, your brain thinks. You might feel always on alert, waiting for the next bit of upsetting news or the next terrible phone call.

It's a good idea to talk to your primary-care provider about any anxiety and feelings of panic, especially if they're pervasive or disabling in any way. Therapy, holistic techniques, and medications, when indicated, can all help. Healing in grief can't begin until you're feeling safe, so it's important to address anxiety as soon as possible.

WHAT TO DO WHEN YOU'RE FEELING VERY ANXIOUS OR PANICKED

Feelings of panic or strong anxiety take over our nervous systems. When this happens, our thoughts race. So do our heartbeats. Our breathing might get faster or labored. We might get clammy or sweaty. We might even feel like we're dying.

If you sometimes feel panicky, it's important to develop a toolkit of strategies that help you calm yourself quickly. Here are a few suggestions:

1. Breathe deeply
   Take slow, deep breaths in through your nose and out through your mouth. Inhale to a count of four then exhale to a count of four.

2. Use your touchstone
   Try carrying a small object that makes you feel grounded and safe, such as a special stone, keepsake, or amulet. When you're feeling panicked, hold it in your hand as you breathe deeply.

3. Lie down and relax your muscles
   As you're breathing deeply, lie down and intentionally focus on moving through your body, relaxing your muscles one at a time.

4. Repeat an affirmation
   Breathe deeply, but instead of counting as you breathe, try repeating an affirmation that comforts you. For example, as you inhale, you could think or say aloud, "I am here," and as you exhale, "I am safe."

5. Go for a walk
   If you're able to, try going for a short walk whenever your anxiety builds. The movement, change of environment, and fresh air will likely clear your heart and mind and restore you to yourself.

SADNESS AND DEPRESSION

Loss and sadness go hand in hand. It's normal to feel the pain of loss. It's also normal to express that pain by crying, wailing, or curling up into a ball.

Sadness can also take the form of a loss of pleasure in life. You might feel deeply sad and hurting, or you might feel more of a numb sadness and lack of interest in things you normally find enjoyable.

In grief, sadness is reconstructive. When we are sad, we instinctively turn inward. We withdraw. We slow down. This instinct to take a time-out from life helps us regroup and acknowledge what has happened. These are necessary steps on the road to healing.

But in grief overload, sadness can become clinical depression. If you've been unable to cope or function day to day, if your grief hasn't eased or changed over a period of months, and/or if your feelings of self-worth are low, you may be suffering from clinical depression in addition to your complicated grief.

If you think you may be clinically depressed—and definitely if you've been entertaining thoughts of suicide—please tell someone who cares about you and also make an appointment with your primary-care provider. As with anxiety (which often accompanies depression), healing in grief can't achieve any momentum until the fog of clinical depression begins to lift.

GUILT AND REGRET

Guilt, regret, and self-blame are natural feelings after significant loss. Normal grief often includes "if-onlys": "If only I had warned him…," "If only I hadn't…," etc. We feel responsible for the people and major attachments in our lives, and when something goes wrong, we may blame ourselves or feel regret about something we did or didn't do.

In grief overload, survivor guilt is a common experience. If multiple people you care about died or suffered in some way, you may understandably wonder why them and not you. You might wish you could take their place but feel the frustration of knowing you can't.

Joy-guilt can arise as well. You may think: How can I possibly feel even intermittent moments of happiness when there has been so much suffering around me?

Guilt and regret are normal feelings in grief that, like all feelings, simply need acknowledgment and exploration. But in grief overload, they can grow weightier and weightier, to the point they may feel crushing.

ANGER AND OTHER EXPLOSIVE EMOTIONS

Anger, hate, blame, resentment, rage, and jealousy are

common in grief. It might help you to understand that these feelings in particular are fundamentally forms of protest. They are a way for you to actively push back against a reality that you do not want to be true. Remember the "fight, flight, or freeze" response I mentioned earlier? Protest emotions are the "fight" option in the trio. It feels better to protest than to give in to the pain of reality.

In grief overload, explosive emotions may be more pronounced, or you may feel stuck in one of them, such as anger. It's understandable to feel angry if you've experienced multiple significant losses. In fact, turning to protest emotions is how you might be surviving your loss overload right now. Yet it's also necessary to find healthy ways to acknowledge and express your anger, so that eventually your anger will soften and stop blocking your other painful emotions, which also need acknowledgment and expression.

RELIEF AND RELEASE

You might be experiencing relief and release as part of your grief overload journey. For example, if a parent or grandparent who suffered with dementia for a long time has died, you may naturally feel sadness and some of the other emotions listed in this section, but you might also feel relieved that the person's suffering is finally over.

Relief is a normal grief feeling, but it can seem like a

contradictory feeling to arise in a situation of grief overload. How it is possible to experience buoyant moments of relief when so many bad things have happened? Relief mixed in with all of the challenging emotions that have been part of your life lately can make you feel even more confused and unsure about how to "do" all your grief.

PHYSICAL SYMPTOMS

Grief affects not only our hearts and minds but also our bodies. The more grief you are dealing with, the more this may be true.

You might feel aches and pains you didn't before. You might be catching germs more easily, since your immune system has likely been weakened by all the stress. You might be having gastrointestinal issues and sleep problems. Other physical symptoms sometimes include an irregular heartbeat, increased blood pressure, blood-sugar imbalances, food cravings or loss of appetite, and clammy skin. These and other bodily symptoms are typical in grief overload. Getting a comprehensive medical check-up is a good idea right now. It can help allay any worries you might have about your own wellness, and it will give you an opportunity to talk to your primary-care doctor about all of your grief-overload symptoms.

COGNITIVE SYMPTOMS

This is a big one in grief overload. Grief always strains thinking skills, because your brain is so distracted by the dismaying new reality it's confronting, but when you are forced to integrate multiple hard-to-believe losses at or around the same time, your brain may not be able to cope. You might find yourself unable to remember simple requests or new information. You may be unable to complete complex (or even simple) tasks. Concentration, short-term memory, and logical processing may seem to have vanished.

The depletion in the brain of the "happy" neurochemicals dopamine and norepinephrine in grief can also wreak cognitive havoc, causing diminished motivation, numbness, fatigue, and an inability to work or complete tasks.

SPIRITUAL SYMPTOMS

I believe that grief is, most of all, a spiritual journey.

In addition to all of the emotional, physical, and cognitive symptoms covered on the previous pages, you are almost certainly (unless you are stuck in numbness) experiencing spiritual symptoms as well. In grief overload, it's common to feel spiritually untethered. You may have had religious or spiritual beliefs that sustained you before, but now you may be questioning some or all of them. After all, as we said, the foundation of your life has been shattered. Or you might be struggling with the reality that you have been subjected to more than your fair share of loss. You may be angry at God. You may be newly searching for God or answers. You may be asking lots of "why?" questions, such as why all of these losses happened. In grief overload, it's natural for "why" questions to precede "how" questions, such as, "How am I going to survive all of this?" All of these spiritual symptoms and more are normal aspects of grief overload.

Your grief has put you in what's called "liminal space." *Limina* is the Latin word for threshold. You are not busily and unthinkingly going about your daily life. Neither is it likely that you are in a place of assuredness about your beliefs. Instead, you are betwixt and between. It's uncomfortable being in liminal space, but that is where grief overload lives.

GRIEF OVERLOAD AND YOUR FAMILY

It's important to keep in mind that all of the aspects of grief overload we're reviewing in this book apply not only to you but also to anyone else in your life who has been affected by the losses.

Each of you is struggling on your own, with your own unique combination of feelings, and if you are a family, you are also struggling together.

In grief overload, each individual has a high need to feel understood and cared for, but a low capacity to be understanding and caring. Remember how we said that grief naturally makes us turn inward? In a family setting, this means that each grieving person has to spend time and energy on themselves before they will be able to turn outward and muster the empathy to spend time and energy on supporting each other.

I urge you to look outside the family for the support each of you needs. Good friends can be lifelines. Other helpers such as spiritual leaders, coaches, and neighbors can also contribute to the network of support. In grief overload, professional grief counseling is another excellent and potentially necessary pillar. Both individual and family counseling will help get your family through this difficult time.

YOUR SIX NEEDS
OF MOURNING

"He wept, and it felt as if the tears were cleansing him,
as if his body needed to empty itself."

— Lois Lowry

We've said that grief is everything you think and feel inside of you about the losses you have suffered.

Mourning, on the other hand, is all of the ways in which you can express your inner grief outside of yourself.

In other words, grief is the inward experience of loss. Mourning is the outward expression of grief.

And active and intentional mourning is how you begin to heal.

Mourning is always necessary in grief, but it's especially necessary in grief overload. Without mourning, the overwhelming, numbing, confusing maelstrom of grief that lives in your heart and mind has nowhere to go. All the tangled thoughts and feelings stay knotted up inside you, essentially roadblocking your path to a satisfying, meaningful, and joyful new life.

But if you open yourself and invite your thoughts and feelings to come out, slowly and over time they begin to untangle. You can see and acknowledge each of them more clearly. You can begin to train your awareness on which precise thoughts and feelings go with which unique loss, and why.

What's more, in allowing your thoughts and feelings to move outside of you, you give them momentum. Mourning is grief in motion. This momentum is what helps you move toward healing.

ONE DOSE AT A TIME

As you work on actively mourning your various griefs, please keep this top of mind: You can only actively mourn in small doses.

Especially in grief overload, it's critical to alternate focusing on your six mourning needs with ample rest and self-care. Mourning is hard, intense, draining work. Do it in small doses, day by day. It's OK to go very slowly. There are no rewards for speed.

So let's talk about mourning now. There are six central mourning needs all grievers have. We'll review some ideas together, and then it will be your sacred work, with the help of a counselor, to try them out and find a combination that works well for you.

GRIEF OVERLOAD AND PROFESSIONAL COUNSELING

Traumatic grief and grief overload are two of the loss circumstances for which I almost always recommend professional counseling.

Even if you have empathetic friends and listeners in your life (and especially if you don't), you need and deserve extra support. I hope you do have close companions that you're able to talk to, because they will also play an important role in your healing. But keep in mind that you may need to share your feelings often, for months and years to come. The magnitude of your grief experience can easily overburden those who are close to you.

What's more, an experienced, compassionate grief counselor can help you create a plan for sorting and mourning the separate losses (see page 41). Each loss will need its own time and attention, and a counselor can help you navigate the process in ways you find helpful and manageable.

1. ACKNOWLEDGE THE REALITY OF THE LOSSES

You have suffered a great deal of loss. I understand that in the face of so much loss, it can be tempting to look away.

It can seem easier not to turn your attention toward the losses and look straight at them. It can seem a better coping strategy to remain in numbness and denial.

Yet as I've said, grief responds to awareness, which is a form of mourning. Identifying the losses contributing to your grief overload and acknowledging their significance in your life is the first step on the road to healing.

While at first you will acknowledge the reality of your losses cognitively, with your head, over time you will begin to acknowledge the reality more and more deeply, with your heart.

Because you are contending with grief overload, I encourage you to talk to at least one trusted listener as well as a professional grief counselor about your losses—in doses and over time. This is not a one-and-done conversation. As long as you are experiencing thoughts and feelings of grief, you will continue to need to talk about your losses.

The good news is that the more you tell the various stories of what happened, the more you will begin to integrate them into a coherent saga of your life. You will be getting to know your own stories better, and you will also be weaving the different threads into a tapestry that starts to feels like a whole.

2. EMBRACE THE PAIN OF THE LOSSES

To reconcile your losses and move toward healing, you must befriend them. You must get to know them and allow yourself to feel whatever feelings arise.

This mourning need seems counterintuitive to many people. After all, our culture teaches us that we deserve to be happy and "move on." But the truth is that we can't find our way back to happiness and a sense of moving forward in life unless we first experience the pain that is an inextricable part of love.

Because that's the truth: your pain *is* your love. Pain is what you feel when you are separated from the object of your love or when a hoped-for future of love and attachment is shattered. Yet even though you are now separated or disconnected from that which you love or hoped for, your love doesn't just stop. Your love goes on. But it's painful because there's nothing but a hole there to receive that particular love. The emptiness hurts. And this hurt is normal and necessary.

And so you must find ways to encounter your pain. Talking with others and your counselor about your losses is one good way, of course. Writing about them in a journal is another. Doing memory work—such as spending time going through photos and memorabilia—is effective for this mourning need, too. Listening to music may help you access your feelings as well.

Yet the pain of grief overload is so great and complicated that you can't embrace it all at once. You can only do it in doses, slowly and over time. You must find ways to intentionally embrace your pain, then intentionally take breaks from your pain. I call this the evade-encounter dance. You will get better at it as you practice it.

MANAGING INTRUSIVE THOUGHTS AND FEELINGS

One of the most exhausting challenges of grief overload can be intrusive thoughts and feelings. Because you are dealing with multiple losses, you might find your mind and heart flitting from one loss to the next throughout the day. Unbidden thoughts and feelings may arise more often than you can handle.

There's a lot to think about and a lot to feel. How do you allow yourself to acknowledge your losses, embrace the pain, and meet your other mourning needs without constantly being waylaid by your grief?

A professional counselor can help you construct a personalized plan that works for you, but my general recommendation to overloaded grievers is to set aside intentional time for active mourning each day. Schedule it into your daily calendar.

Then, when a thought or feeling arises, which will happen, allow yourself to feel it for just a moment then jot down a note about it in a notebook that you keep for this purpose. In other words, give the thought or feeling a moment of attention, and promise it that you will return to it during the appointed mourning time you've scheduled into your daily calendar.

You cannot control your thoughts and feelings, but you can work toward finding ways to both mourn and live at the same time. In the early weeks and months of your most intense grief, you may need to devote most of your time to mourning. But as time passes and you begin to return to regular activities, it works well for most people to allow themselves to experience their grief for dedicated bits of time then step away from it. At other times you may need to put your active mourning on hold for a short while, in order to get through another life demand. That's OK, too, as long as you don't defer for too long.

---

3. REMEMBER THE PEOPLE WHO DIED AND THE THINGS YOU LOST
In grief overload, remembering is often particularly painful. After all, as we've already acknowledged, the circumstances that gave rise to all the grief are difficult at best and at times gut-wrenchingly traumatic. (Here I want to reiterate that if you're struggling with traumatic grief (see page 4), you are wise to seek the support of a skilled, experienced grief counselor, especially as you do the mourning work of encountering memories that may be intertwined with violence, abuse, or other extreme situations.)

Yet one of the paradoxes of grief is that remembering the past is what makes hoping for the future possible. And like the first two mourning needs—acknowledging the reality and embracing the pain of the losses—actively encountering memories is essential.

I'll say it again: grief responds to awareness. Part of your grief work right now is turning your awareness to your memories, both good and bad. Of course, each loss you are grieving has its own cache of memories, so you will need to devote time to remembering each lost person or attachment separately.

As with befriending your feelings, befriending your memories tends to tame them. Memories become less powerful and all-consuming when you talk about them, write about them, make art about them, create photo books and memory boxes about them, and express them in other ways.

Ultimately, active remembering is about integrating your past with your present and future. They are all parts of the story of your one, singular life, and they all belong.

4. DEVELOP A NEW SELF-IDENTITY

The people, pets, places, and things we love are all parts of our self-identities.

I'm a husband and father. I'm also a son, a brother, an uncle, a friend—and soon to be a grandfather! I'm a professional speaker and author, too. And I'm a dog dad, a car buff, a hiker, a Coloradan, and more. All of these aspects of my life are part of my self-identity. When any of them are threatened or severed in any way, this leaves a big hole that forces me to patch myself up and make myself anew.

You are a person who has experienced extensive loss, which means that your self-identity has suffered many blows. You may feel full of holes right now. Patching yourself up into a new whole will be hard but worthwhile work. Another way to think of it is that your connections in life are mirrors in which you see yourself—and now you have lost too many mirrors. This can create a feeling of "identity diffusion."

Who are you now? Who are you no longer? What have you been forced to leave behind? What have you chosen to leave behind? How have your losses shaped you? How have your joys shaped you? What do you see for yourself moving forward? Actively seeking out, pondering, and expressing your thoughts and feelings about these questions is what this mourning need is all about.

As you work to mourn your various griefs, you will find that each loss affected your self-identity in its own unique ways. It's normal and necessary to explore all of these facets.

Support groups focused on a certain type of loss can be an excellent forum for exploring self-identity changes related to that type of loss. In-person support groups are excellent, but online support groups for less common loss types can also be extremely effective. And don't forget to reach out to others in your life who have suffered a similar loss. If you are a recent widow, for example, it is likely that other widows you know have wisdom and compassion to share.

Other ways of actively mourning your old self-identity and developing a new one include discussing your thoughts and feelings with friends, reading books about self-development and journaling your responses, and trying out new avenues of self-exploration. Which relationships, careers, volunteer roles, hobbies, and activities are calling to you? Give awareness to this call, and answer it with action.

5. SEARCH FOR MEANING

In grief, it's normal to try to make sense of what happened, and it's necessary to find things that give your changed life continued meaning.

After each loss you've experienced, you've probably found yourself wondering why it had to happen. Why this loss? Why now? Why in this way? You may not always arrive at satisfactory answers to such questions, but still, it's normal to ask them.

Some of your questions may have to do with the specific details of a loss and the events leading up to the loss. If you want to know more about the particulars of what happened and why, I urge to you to pursue these answers. If you don't, you may feel stuck, and it will be harder for you to move forward in your grief. What's more, actively seeking out information and answers helps meet this mourning need.

Other questions are more esoteric and spiritual in nature. Why do bad things happen to good people? Why does God allow so much pain in human life? What is the meaning of life? Your religious, spiritual, and philosophical beliefs come into play here, of course.

As I said earlier, grief is fundamentally a spiritual journey, and so exploring the spiritual aspects of your grief is perhaps your most essential mourning task. You do this by making regular time for spiritual work—every day, if possible. Find ways to step outside your daily demands and get in touch with your spirit.

For some people, this means visiting a place of worship or praying each day. Others find spiritual presence and connection in meditation, spending time in nature, and other contemplative practices. Talking to spiritual mentors, taking spiritual courses, and listening to spiritual podcasts are additional avenues.

Simultaneously, it's essential to find reasons to keep getting out of bed in the morning and rebuild hope for the future.

Scheduling little treats and respites into each day—helping balance the pain of active mourning—is a good idea. And for the long-term, you can't go wrong if you start taking steps toward activities and relationships that give you a sense of meaning and purpose.

6. RECEIVE ONGOING SUPPORT FROM OTHERS

The final need of mourning is to reach out for and receive ongoing support from your fellow human beings. This is a critical need when you are faced with grief overload.

We all need and deserve connection with others. In fact, close human relationships are arguably the most meaningful experiences in life. In times of great grief, however, these relationships become even more essential because you must rely on other people to help hold you up.

Consider what makes you feel most loved and supported, and seek out that type of interaction. You might want to talk about your losses to caring listeners a great deal. Or you might want to talk less but instead simply spend time with others. Or perhaps you're someone who feels especially supported when people write you words of encouragement, in cards, emails, and texts. Of course, a combination of all these kinds of support may be just right!

Not everyone has the capacity to be a good friend in grief,

however. Most people have been shaped by our grief-avoiding culture, which prefers to deny or bottle up grief. But some people in your life—about one-third, in my experience—likely have the listening skills and empathy it takes to be present to you whenever you need to express what's in your mind and on your heart. Another third are typically neutral when it comes to grief support; they neither help nor hinder you. And the final third can be toxic. These are the people who shame you, deplete your energy with their own dramas, or make you feel judged or dismissed. Avoid this last group as much as possible. And remember that even the first group can become overwhelmed by the magnitude of your losses.

So even if you have some strongly empathetic friends and family, I encourage you to seek extra help. In situations of loss overload, grief support is best supplemented by professional counseling and support-group participation. Understandably, you have a lot of grief to express. And it may take months and possibly years of active, engaged, committed mourning for you to feel that your grief is being reconciled and you are achieving momentum toward a present and future of meaning and purpose. So please look into counseling and support groups if you haven't already. I promise you that both will be a lifeline in helping you get from here to there.

MAKING A
MOURNING PLAN

*"We must embrace the pain and
use it as fuel for our journey."*
— Kenji Miyazawa

Once you've identified all of the losses, past and present, that
may be contributing to your grief overload, it's time to create
a plan to mourn them. One of the trickiest aspects of grief
overload is figuring out how to mourn (express outside of
yourself) everything that needs mourning.

As I've said, one of the things a professional grief counselor
can do for you is help you create a strategy and plan for
mourning your various losses. It's really overwhelming—
indeed, I would say impossible—to mourn all the aspects of
all the losses all at once. So I generally recommend setting
aside mourning times and activities for each unique loss.
In other words, each loss demands and deserves individual
attention.

MY MOURNING PLAN

I invite you to use this chart as you're beginning to think about ways to mourn each unique loss that is part of your grief overload. Consider secondary losses as well as primary losses.

Write your losses in the top row. Then in each blank box, or some of the blank boxes, jot down an idea that helps meet the mourning need in the left column for that loss. Be specific. And don't forget that you'll need to dose your active mourning.

	Loss:
1. Acknowledging the reality	
2. Embracing the pain	
3. Remembering	
4. Developing a new self-identity	
5. Searching for meaning	
6. Receiving support from others	
Other notes	

Too Much Loss: Coping with Grief Overload

You might consider working on one box for half an hour or an hour one day, then returning to your normal routine. If you do this most days of the week, you will find yourself gaining momentum toward reconciliation and healing.

I suggest making blank copies of this grid and filling out a new one each month or so to help you navigate your healing journey.

Loss:	Loss:	Loss:

For example, if one of the losses you're mourning is the death of someone special, I might suggest that you start working on a memory book or box for that individual person. Once or twice a week, for an hour or so each session, you could assemble photos and other memorabilia in a special scrapbook or box. You could invite someone else to help you, or it could be a solo activity. In addition to gathering and sorting the objects, you could also take the time to write a little note to accompany each item, perhaps with details such as the date or occasion associated with the item, and anything else that you feel is important. Each time you sit down to focus on an activity such as this, you are opening your heart to this particular loss.

This one-at-a-time technique applies to other mourning activities as well.

- If you're seeing a counselor, you might suggest that particular meetings focus on particular losses sometimes.

- A certain in-person support group might help you acknowledge and embrace one unique loss, while a different online support group might help you with another.

- If journaling feels like an effective way to explore loss for you, you could dedicate one journal to each loss.

- Spending time in a specific location can help you mourn a specific loss.

- You get the idea!

I don't mean to imply that you can totally sort and compartmentalize each unique grief, of course. Grief is a spiritual and emotional experience, and while it responds to awareness, it can't really be controlled with logic.

So even as you're dedicating time and attention to mourn a particular loss, other thoughts, feelings, and memories will probably creep in…and that's OK. You will likely find yourself going back and forth among the various losses. When that happens, acknowledge them then return to what you were doing.

And please be self-compassionate if you feel overwhelmed at any point in the mourning process. You may not know where to begin. You may not know where to go next. Be gentle with yourself, and adjust your expectations about both the intensity and duration of this naturally complicated experience.

Also, remember that your mourning plan is an ever-changing work in progress. Certain losses will weigh more heavily at certain times, such as anniversaries, birthdays, and holidays. At those times, losses tied to those dates will probably need more attention. And when particular thoughts and feelings dominate, that means they need more attention at that moment, too.

Trust your grief. Listen to it. Learn from it. Allow it to lead and teach you—at its own pace—what it needs. You will eventually experience a sense of self-direction as you give attention to your mourning.

RECONCILING
YOUR GRIEF

*"You will heal, and you will rebuild yourself around
the loss you have suffered. You will be whole again,
but you will never be the same."*
— Elisabeth Kübler-Ross

We don't "get over" grief. We don't forget our losses. Instead, if we mourn them well, our losses become part of who we are. We reconcile ourselves to them, and we learn changed ways of living forward with meaning and purpose even as we continue to grieve and often love what was left behind.

You'll know that you're beginning to achieve some reconciliation of your losses when you start to feel better. Lighter. Your thoughts and feelings of grief will begin to seem softer and gentler. They won't arise as often, and they won't take over your mood and attention as forcefully or as often. You'll begin to feel more energetic and hopeful. Watch for these signs of healing as you engage with your grief.

In grief overload, reconciliation takes time—often a great

deal of time. Yes, grief responds beautifully to awareness and active mourning, but it also takes months and sometimes years for the various griefs to feel well integrated into your continued living. This is normal.

I urge you to be patient and gentle with yourself along the way. There is no deadline. There is not always forward motion. Sometimes it may feel like you're going backward. But the sooner and more often you devote yourself to active mourning, the sooner you are likely to find yourself soothed by the balm of reconciliation.

I've also mentioned healing a number of times in this book. Healing in grief means to become whole again. Remember how I said that loss creates holes inside us? It's the process of active mourning that helps us patch up those holes—yet something that's patched is not the same as it was before, is it? It's changed. It's new and different.

Your reconciled grief will transform you into a new and different person. You may wish things could be as they were before, but they cannot. And so your goal becomes working your way toward a new normal that feels whole and purposeful. Many grievers ultimately discover exciting, joyful, courageous, and honorable new parts of themselves in this process.

A FINAL WORD

*"I have been sustained throughout my life
by three saving graces—my family, my friends,
and a faith in the power of resilience and hope."*
— Elizabeth Edwards

Grief overload is a very real and challenging problem in your life. It's also a significant public-health issue. The good news is that in recent years, we as a culture have been getting a little better about recognizing and talking openly about grief and the need to mourn. Some of the stigma is lifting.

I am hopeful for your healing. I hope you are too. I encourage you to intentionally jumpstart and nurture your own hopefulness. How do you nurture hope? By spending time with the people and pets you love. By taking part in activities you care about. By regularly prioritizing and engaging in spiritual practices. By making future plans that excite you. By building daily pleasures into your schedule— and relishing them. By helping others. By taking care of your body, mind, heart, social connections, and soul.

The more you nurture your spark of hope, the more it will grow. The spark will become a flame, and the flame can become a fire. And even on days when the fire temporarily ebbs and fades to embers, you'll know that you have the power to rebuild it again in all of the ways listed above.

I wish you authentic grief and mourning in the months and years ahead. I also wish you hope and healing. I believe in your capacity to reconcile your griefs and live forward with joy and purpose. Godspeed.

COPING WITH GRIEF OVERLOAD: THE MOURNER'S BILL OF RIGHTS

Though you should reach out to others as you do the work of mourning, you should not feel obligated to accept the unhelpful responses you may receive from some people. You are the one who is grieving, and as such, you have certain "rights" no one should try to take away from you.

1. *You have the right to experience your own unique grief.*
   Your grief is unique. What's more, your grief for each individual loss is unique. So, when you turn to others for help, don't allow them to tell you what you should or should not be feeling. And try not to judge others for how they are grieving, either.

2. *You have the right to talk about your grief.*
   Talking about your various losses will help you heal. Seek out others who will allow you to share your stories with them. In grief overload, the listening ears of a compassionate professional counselor are also essential. If at times you don't feel like talking, you also have the right to be silent—just don't remain silent for too long.

3. *You have the right to feel a multitude of emotions.*
   Shock, anger, fear, guilt, and relief are just a few of the
   emotions you might experience as part of your grief
   journey. None of your feelings are wrong, but all need to
   be expressed. Find ways to acknowledge and express each
   feeling for each loss.

4. *You have the right to make healing in grief a top priority.*
   Understandably, grief overload tends to make people feel
   overwhelmed, dragged down, and stuck. By prioritizing
   active mourning in your life, you will be giving yourself
   the emotional and spiritual intensive care you need to get
   unstuck and rise up again.

5. *You have the right to be tolerant of your physical and*
   emotional limits.
   Your feelings of loss and sadness will probably leave you
   feeling fatigued. Respect what your body and mind are
   telling you. Get daily rest. Eat balanced meals. And don't
   allow others to push you into doing things you don't feel
   ready to do. Go as slowly as you need to. There are no
   rewards for speed.

6. *You have the right to experience "griefbursts."*
   Sometimes, out of nowhere, powerful surges of grief
   may overcome you. These can be frightening, but they
   are normal and natural. Work on strategies to calm and
   soothe yourself when this happens.

7. *You have the right to embrace your spirituality.*
   Express your religious or spiritual beliefs and questions
   in ways that feel right to you. Allow yourself to be around
   people who understand and support your religious or
   spiritual beliefs.

8. *You have the right to search for meaning.*
   You may find yourself asking questions such as, "Why
   did these things happen? Why in this way?" Some of your
   questions may have answers, but some may not. Watch
   out for the clichéd responses some people may give you.
   Comments like "It was God's will" or "Think of what you
   still have to be thankful for" are not helpful, and you do
   not have to accept them.

9. *You have the right to treasure good memories.*
   Happy memories are one of the best legacies that exist
   after significant loss. You will always remember. Instead of
   ignoring your memories, find ways to express and share
   them.

10. *You have the right to move toward your grief and heal.*
    Reconciling your losses will not happen quickly.
    Remember, grief is a process, not an event. Be patient
    and tolerant with yourself, and avoid people who are
    impatient and intolerant with you. Yet also remember that
    active mourning is your ally and your power. Intentionally
    engaging with the six needs of mourning is what will carry
    you toward your grief and help you heal.

The Journey Through Grief
REFLECTIONS ON HEALING | SECOND EDITION

This revised, second edition of *The Journey Through Grief* takes Dr. Wolfelt's popular book of reflections and adds space for guided journaling, asking readers thoughtful questions about their unique mourning needs and providing room to write responses.

ISBN 978-1-879651-11-1 • 152 pages • hardcover • $21.95

First Aid for Broken Hearts

Life is both wonderful and devastating. It graces us with joy, and it breaks our hearts. If your heart is broken, this book is for you. Whether you're struggling with a death, break-up, illness, unwanted life change, or loss of any kind, this book will help you both understand your predicament and figure out what to do about it.

ISBN: 978-1-61722-281-8 • softcover • $9.95

The Wilderness of Grief
A BEAUTIFUL, HARDCOVER GIFT BOOK VERSION OF
UNDERSTANDING YOUR GRIEF

The Wilderness of Grief is an excerpted version of *Understanding Your Grief*, making it approachable and appropriate for all mourners. This concise book makes an excellent gift for anyone in mourning. On the book's inside front cover is room for writing an inscription to your grieving friend.

ISBN 978-1-879651-52-4 • 112 pages • hardcover • $15.95

All Dr. Wolfelt's publications can be ordered by mail from:
Companion Press, 3735 Broken Bow Road, Fort Collins, CO 80526
(970) 226-6050 • www.centerforloss.com

NOTES:

NOTES:

NOTES:

NOTES:

ABOUT THE AUTHOR

Alan D. Wolfelt, Ph.D., is a respected author and educator on the topics of companioning others and healing in grief. He serves as Director of the Center for Loss and Life Transition and is on the faculty at the University of Colorado Medical

School's Department of Family Medicine. Dr. Wolfelt has written many bestselling books on healing in grief, including *Understanding Your Grief*, *Healing Your Grieving Heart*, and *The Mourner's Book of Hope*. Visit www.centerforloss.com to learn more about grief and loss and to order Dr. Wolfelt's books.